Late Pickings

Gavin Ewart

HUTCHINSON

London Melbourne Auckland Johannesburg

© Gavin Ewart 1987

This edition first published in 1987 by Hutchinson Ltd,
an imprint of Century Hutchinson Ltd,
Brookmount House, 62–65 Chandos Place, London WC2N 4NW

Century Hutchinson Australia Pty Ltd
PO Box 496, 16–22 Church Street, Hawthorn, Victoria 3122, Australia

Century Hutchinson New Zealand Limited
PO Box 40-086, Glenfield, Auckland 10, New Zealand

Century Hutchinson South Africa (Pty) Ltd
PO Box 337, Bergvlei, 2012 South Africa

Photoset by Rowland Phototypesetting Ltd
Bury St Edmunds, Suffolk
Printed and bound in Great Britain by
The Guernsey Press, Guernsey

British Library Cataloguing in Publication Data

Ewart, Gavin
Late pickings.
I. Title
821'.912   PR6055.W3

ISBN 0-09-168251-7

For Lincoln Kirstein

Thank-you Letter
(Connecticut, 22 June 1985)

Hotel-'n-houseguest, I must pay
with words the wind won't blow away –
   classic in style (like Philip Johnson),
   not like mad Rolfe*. Call Benson Bonsen,

he thought, was disguise enough
to stop wise lawyers getting tough.
   His ingratitude then led him
   to bite hard the hand that fed him.

I am of a different sort.
Was he sherry? Then I'm port.
   Not alone for food and drinking,
   but for thoughts that were worth thinking

and for expertise in arts
that involve both heads and hearts
   I must thank you! We are nurslings
   of the Muse; and your steel verslings,

like scalpels probing, can excise
urban horrors from our eyes,
   not by gentling, smoothing, blanding,
   but increasing understanding.

* See *The Desire and Pursuit of the Whole* by Frederick Rolfe, a very eccentric Catholic who thought he ought to be Pope. The unpleasant character of 'Bonsen' in this auto-biographical novel is based on Mgr Robert Hugh Benson, one of Rolfe's benefactors.

5

Also, as you love to do,
showing *objets de vertu*
    is as good as wining-dining,
    lessening my Philistining

unawareness of what paint,
downing Devil, serving Saint,
    can do with its exorcism
    of Greed's heresy and schism.

Art is harmless, art's a game;
but it's potent, all the same.
    Life's enjoying or enduring
    (Dr Johnson was assuring)

can be helped along by it.
This we understand a bit.
    Cricketers rave about leg-glancers,
    you about the agile dancers.

Thanks are thanks, and thanks are due
most especially to you.
    Accept them therefore from a punier,
    by no means ungrateful junior!

Contents

ACKNOWLEDGMENTS

Some of the poems in this book have appeared in the following publications: *Ambit, Bananas, British Book News, Country Life, Edinburgh Review, Encounter, Grand Street* (USA), *Light Year 87* (Bits Press, USA), *Literary Review, London Magazine, New Democrat, New Directions, New Edinburgh Review, New Poetry 10, New Statesman* (Competition), *Nine New Poems* (Bits Press, USA), *Poetry Australia, Poetry Book Society Supplement 1986, Poetry Nation, Poetry Review, Strawberry Fare, The Honest Ulsterman, The Listener, The Paris Review* (USA), *The Salmon* (Galway), *The Sunday Times, The Times Literary Supplement*.

Introduction

These poems of my old age are called 'Late Pickings' because of the German wine harvest. Some grapes are not picked until very late in the year, sometimes even after there have been frosts. Wines made from these grapes are known for their sweetness and grapey flavour; they have the generic name of *Spätlese* (a late picking) and are among the most prized white wines. One of them is actually called an *Eiswein* (ice-wine), when the gathering of the grapes has been left so late that ice has actually formed round them, concentrating the sweetness. The title was chosen with reference to the time of collecting – and not to the quality or nature of the poems.

Anybody who writes a lot of rhyming verse always runs the risk of repeating rhymes. I must warn all readers who are sensitive to this kind of thing that in two separate poems 'Noddy' is rhymed with 'body' and 'Noddy's' with 'bodies'.

Part One

The Sadness of Cricket

many facts from *The Golden Age of Cricket 1890–1914*
by David Frith

The happy summer game, where fun
lies like a playful cat in golden sun –
true innocence in every ball and every run –

where all is for the best, they say,
nostalgia only when it goes away –
romantic memories that haunt the close of play –

is like that poem, 'Dover Beach',
like Arnold's lovely world it's out of reach,
and there are other lessons it might also teach.

How golden lads of Housman's sort
lose all that beauty and can end up caught –
by portliness – and far too fond of gin and port.

And how the agile cover point
slows with arthritis in each stiffened joint –
his briskest fielding now would only disappoint.

Those godlike carefree flashing blades
don't flash for ever in that field of shades
and time can trump a Trumper like an ace of spades.

All right for private incomes, turn
to them they could, money they had to burn,
the amateurs, the Gentlemen! But Players earn

their living in a young man's game –
when they retire it's never quite the same.
If they despaired, would they be very much to blame?

15

Coaches and pros at public schools,
they taught the rudiments to flannelled fools;
like swimmers striking out in private swimming pools,

the young were trained in all the strokes.
But did *they* feel like victims of a hoax?
Famous fast bowlers, run to fat, now schoolboy jokes?

We'd one at Wellington, that A. E. Relf,
who'd bowled for England – since long on the shelf –
in 1937 stalled and shot himself.

Remembered bowling in the nets,
a little irritable (I thought – but one forgets),
doling out stumps to junior games, like doubtful debts,

from the Pavilion's mean back door.
He had this job, I wouldn't think him poor,
but losing it might put him firmly on the floor.

Professionals lose jobs? They could.
Respectful, yes, you had to be – and 'good'.
Some amateurs cut loose, but it was understood

that there was really no appeal
(although it seems to me a dodgy deal)
when Players misbehaved; witness the case of Peel,

a Yorkshire bowler, too content
to stay in the beer tent, his favourite tent.
A Test Match bowler too, but did Lord Hawke relent?

Peed on the pitch! A County game
was scene of his unheard-of drunken shame.
Hawke threw him out; and Peel's a long-forgotten name.

Pro with a County? Umpire? Then
that was 'retirement' for such humble men.
Cricket Schools? Sports goods? These were rare in 1910.

Though Gunn made bats. The 'Autograph'
by Gunn & Moore, his sporting epitaph.
Used once by me. My batting, though, would make you laugh.

Strength, talent gone – then what to do?
Great Albert Trott, like Relf, was gunned down too
by his own hand in Willesden – very sad but true.

'His powers waned in 1904'
the record says – and just £4, no more,
was found, his wardrobe left to landlady. The score

of that fine bowler/batsman: small.
'He liked a pint'; but dropsy took it all.
In 1914 – thousands more about to fall –

Harry Graham and Johnny Briggs
died in asylums – and among the prigs
who wouldn't fancy Burns (corn rigs and barley rigs)

you might count batsman A. E. Knight,
'mental' perhaps, at least not over-bright,
who prayed while batting – an extraordinary sight!

And Arthur Shrewsbury, tipped by Grace
as runner-up in the Great Batsman Race –
he was a suicide. He couldn't stand the pace;

thousands of runs that he amassed
made Grace a generous enthusiast
but didn't help. And Aubrey Faulkner, too, was gassed

in London, 1930, by
his own sad hand. It makes you want to cry –
but all they wanted was some peace, simply to die.

And Arthur Woodcock also went,
in 1910, by his own poison sent
to that far bourne. Each cricket season was lent

17

to Leicestershire. He coached the lads
at an American College; and their Dads
remembered him as fast as Kortright. Oiks and cads

such may have been. At 44
he thought it time to leave and shut the door . . .
The Gentlemen had deaths as well, but in the War.

Poor Stoddart was another case,
who shared great opening partnerships with Grace –
but shot himself at 52. Life's hard to face!

The blazer and the ribboned coat?
The most pathetic soul for Charon's boat
was Percy Frederick Hardy – he just cut his throat

at King's Cross Station; old and mean,
the Fates attacked him, March 1916.
Ten years for Somerset, a useful pro, he'd been

scared of the Front, the shells, the mud.
A public lavatory received his blood.
The County of London Yeomanry found him a dud.

The Captains toss. It's Heads or Tails;
but Time and Death at last remove the bails,
though you weep buckets of the Bard's prophetic pails.

You can work gents into the mix.
George Lohmann died (T.B.) at 36,
and Alfred Lyttelton was himself hit for six –

an abscess from a cricket ball,
a Cabinet Minister when toffs walked tall.
A famous Foster was most interesting of all –

one of the Worcester brothers who
made Worcester Fostershire, and rightly too.
Down in the world he went, an easy thing to do.

A tart was murdered, and police
knew that he knew her. Questions didn't cease,
frequent as cigarette burns on a mantelpiece.

He took her home (200 fags,
a bottle of Scotch whisky bought – old bags
like this) but she was young and not the kind that nags.

At 20 Nora Upchurch had
gone loose in London – also to the bad.
Strangled in Shaftesbury Avenue (that's also trad).

An empty house. A man called Field
confessed to Press, and all was then 'revealed'
that for two years had been quite well concealed.

'Not guilty' at Old Bailey (he
retracted all he'd said), in '33
he walked away, he was released, completely free.

But later tried the same trick twice.
This time the jury turned out not so nice.
You win some, lose some, it's the shaking of the dice.

Nobody gets away with much.
Even late cuts, the Ranjitsinhji touch,
leg glances, don't impress the Fates and gods and such.

A Gorgon married C. B. Fry.
Call no man lucky till he's come to die;
So said the Greeks, and they had ancient reasons why.

NOTES

1 *Victor Trumper (1877–1915)* One of the greatest Australian batsmen.
Like Grace and Hobbs, he could make high scores on very difficult
wickets. He died at the age of 35.

19

2 *Bobby Peel*   Yorkshire bowler (Yorkshire won the County Championship nine times between 1893 and 1912). He took 102 Test wickets against Australia; once winning a Test by ten runs (taking 8 for 67) but had to be sobered up in a cold shower beforehand by his Captain.

3 *William Gunn*   A great Nottinghamshire and England batsman (George Gunn was his only slightly less famous brother). In 1896 he went on strike, refusing to play in a Test team unless he was paid £20, instead of the usual £10. He died a wealthy man – because of his partnership in Gunn & Moore.

4 *Albert Trott*   An Australian bowler with several styles, and a tremendous hitter. He took 8 for 43 in his first Test against England. When the selectors ignored him, he played as a pro for Middlesex (4 wickets in 4 balls and later a hat-trick against Somerset, in his benefit match in 1907). In 1899 and 1900 made over 1,000 runs, took 200 wickets in each season. An umpire in 1910.

5 *Albert Knight*   Went to Australia with P. F. Warner's team of 1903–04. He is slandered in the poem, since he was apparently 'thoughtful and well-read'. Nevertheless the Lancashire fast bowler Walter Brearley is supposed to have reported him to the M.C.C. for praying during an innings.

6 *Arthur Shrewsbury*   The greatest professional batsman of the 1880s and 1890s. His 164 on a dangerous pitch in the Lord's Test of 1886, against the bowling of Spofforth, is reckoned one of the finest innings ever played. He was an opening batsman of extraordinary patience. He captained England in seven Tests in Australia. Committed suicide in 1903, aged 47.

7 *Aubrey Faulkner*   A South African Test cricketer, who also played for the Gentlemen. Very successful in the 1909–10 series against England. A D.S.O. in the War.

8 *Arthur Woodcock*   Described as 'a magnificent specimen of Midlands manhood'. Kortright was the fastest bowler of his day, and at his best Woodcock was thought to be as fast.

9 *A. E. Stoddart*   Captain of England at cricket and rugby. While leading England in the 1894–95 tour, he made 173 at Melbourne – highest score by an England captain in Australia until 1975. In his last match for Middlesex in 1900 he scored 221. His opening partnerships with

W. G. Grace were legendary. He shot himself in 1915, soon after his 52nd birthday.

10 *Percy Frederick Hardy*   He was a Dorset-born left-hander, but played for Somerset. Top score: 91 against Kent at Taunton in 1910.

11 *George Lohmann*   One of the 'strikers' of 1896, and a principal professional bowler for Surrey. Took 100 wickets, for example, in 1892 – when Surrey were Champions for the third year running.

12 *Alfred Lyttleton*   Brother-in-law of Arthur Balfour, Prime Minister. Wicket-keeper batsman for Eton, Cambridge, Middlesex, Worcestershire, the Gentlemen and England. In 1884, in a Test at the Oval, he removed his wicket-keeper's pads and took 4 for 19 with underarm lobs. In 1913, when he was 56, a blow from the ball caused an internal abscess – from which he died.

13 *The Fosters*   There were seven Foster brothers, sons of a Malvern clergyman. R. E. ('Tip') Foster made two centuries at Lord's in his first appearance for the Gentlemen. He was the only brother to play for England (287 in his first Test v. Australia, 1903–04). He captained England in South Africa (1907). Once hit W. G. Grace for four consecutive sixes. Died of diabetes in 1914, aged 36. For details of the Field case, see *A Reasonable Doubt* by Julian Symons.

14 *K. S. Ranjitsinhji*   The famous Indian Prince who played for Cambridge, Sussex and England. A great stylist, he was the first man to score 3,000 runs in a season.

15 *C. B. Fry*   The blue-eyed boy. Scholar, athlete, footballer (Association and Rugby Union), journalist, Naval officer, schoolmaster. Played for Sussex and England. Six successive First Class centuries in 1901 (still a record). Married Beatrice Sumner, a very tough lady who (after his death) took over command of a training ship for Royal Naval cadets, forbidding all masturbation, dumb insolence and answering back.

A Murder and a Suicide in Wartime

You'd think neither was necessary,
with so many soldiers being killed –
the German, the Italian, the Russian brother –
but I came across the one
and then the other.

In 1942 the Troop was in billets,
not long before we went overseas,
Fernhurst or Fleet (I think the latter),
the memory blurs, and finally
that's no great matter . . .

There was one Welsh gunner
always being picked on by a Bombardier
for Welshness and stupidity;
this irked him like pre-thunder
pressured humidity,

so one night he took an axe
(part of the standard Fire Precautions)
as everyone lay peacefully sleeping.
Heavy strokes, blood splashing,
running and seeping,

he bashed the Lance-Bombardier's
handsome unconscious head in . . .
was he paranoid or persecuted?
At least authoritarian niggling
was more than muted.

The suicide happened in North Africa –
a big, apparently happy, gunner
shot himself with his own rifle.
What triggered that, what depression
or magnified trifle?

They said he was happily married.
Would the separation cause it?
The MO's death certificate hit one nail
on the head: in perfect health,
the body of a young male . . .

Tribes

('Here's tae us – wha's like us?')

Are tribes a good thing?
Or are they bad, and ugly –
as smugly they hug themselves
over a victory, football or cricket
or almost anything?

Irish, Welsh or Scots –
should they pride themselves so
on Kelso? do they smell so
terrifically sweet? what about their feet?
English, Irish, Welsh or Scots?

You could pride yourself
on looking like Cardinal Newman,
on being a woman or human
or deft or left-handed, or 'gentry' or 'landed'.
You *could* pride yourself.

But it's all a bit fake,
a bit bogus and silly –
a big willie, being a hillbilly,
most pride is foolish, stubborn and mulish
but in the end a bit fake!

The Brewery Tap

'Theer's no reet lass works in a pub!'
This was a Yorkshire dictum
from before the War (I did Market Research) –
and certainly landlords picked them

for blousy bosoms that charmed the lads
and real or bogus blondeness.
The regulars were bold of speech,
with a certain routine fondness,

fancying themselves as connoisseurs,
as choosers and pickers.
There were jokes about tin-openers too,
the futility of tin knickers.

Barmaids took them as compliments,
predictable and predicted.
It never went further than 'Gi'e us a kiss!'
The love-making was restricted

to what could be done in a Public Bar
without appearing shocking –
though male minds had their suspender belts
and the silkiness of a stocking.

They all equated Sex with Sin,
with naughty Eve and her apple,
and Drink was the third in that Trinity
in every Methodist Chapel.

The Brewery Tap is at the source,
where they knock one p. off the bitter,
where Satan is busy pulling the pints
and Sin bears her yelping litter

(it's all there, plain, in *Paradise Lost*) –
it's a wicked Garden of Eden,
a real-life Cockaigne where the Lord is mocked,
a sweltering sex-mad Sweden.

That was the theory. But fifty years
have made it all seem cosy;
the future of Sin in those Public Bars
isn't, now, quite so rosy.

There are fights of course, and boys and girls
can start being alcoholic –
but a glass of beer isn't filled with fear
and it isn't truly symbolic

of Wickedness and the Fall of Man.
The long slow pints of the Pensioner
are innocent things – and as for Sin,
there's not much reason to mention her.

She's out on the streets, where the pushers are,
baiting the teenage trap.
Big H, cocaine – it's a world away
from the simple Brewery Tap.

NOTE   'The Brewery Tap' is a Young's pub in
Wandsworth, part of the brewery (hence the lower price). In
Paradise Lost Sin is described as the mother of Death –
Satan was the father.

26

Dying

How wonderful, how lovely, if you could just
come romping up on a charger,
in victorious armour,
with all the trumpets blowing!

How marvellous, how rewarding, if you just
broke the tape, with everyone cheering,
'What style! What daring!'
and all that triumphant shouting!

How consolatory, even, how right, how just,
the sentimental 'cellos sadly mourning
with their mellow moaning,
like TV or a sad film running!

How mistaken! For hours the just and the unjust
lie on the battlefield severely wounded
and no trumpet is sounded,
no 'cello plays for them as they lie dying!

24th March 1986

Thirty long years have passed away
since that most auspicious day –
   black and white, the photos tell
   all but the temperature and smell

(and the colour), ikons rich
in that peculiar feeling which
   makes us think – then think again.
   Stroll with me down Memory Lane

is what the simple souls pronounce
whose pound of flesh is, every ounce,
   cut from the body of the Past.
   And yet a union that can last

for so long isn't incidental
(though pleasing to the sentimental).
   Marriages fade, and slide and slip,
   but you can bet a partnership

that's lasted now for three decades
deserves poetic accolades!
   No need to be a solemn owl
   to tell us how fair winds and foul

can blow on marriages, that tack
between 'Oh, love!' and 'Take that back!'
   Romeo and Juliet too
   had their bad moments (although few).

The path of true love isn't smooth,
the ruffled feathers sex can soothe
   ruffle again – for couples never
   spend all their lives in bed together.

So, camera-caught, I'm standing there,
the March wind bullying my hair,
    with you half-serious at my side
    in the doll's clothes that mark a bride.

Would I have known, would I have thought, too,
that such 'Till Deathness' could or ought to,
    holy or not, a close communion,
    be such a feature of our union?

Nobody knows what's on its way —
we all get by, from day to day —
    but it's a marvel, plain to see,
    that you should stay so long with me!

'Love me little, love me long!' —
No. Love grows different, but grows strong,
    and time can change it to its best
    by subtle compound interest.

The Old Deaths

In the Twenties, when I was ten or more,
my mother used to tell me about the deaths of old people –
perhaps this was to forestall questions like:
'Why don't we go to see Aunt Annie any more?'

She would say, 'You remember old Mrs Something?
Well, she's died.' There were never any details –
as now, being grown-up, we might easily say
'It was cancer of the larynx,' or something of the something.

I never asked. I wasn't very curious.
Dying, like smoking, was a thing that grown-ups did.
Let them get on with it, would be roughly my attitude.
I accepted it as part of life; it wasn't odd or curious.

Aunt Annie lived close, among Eastern souvenirs –
she had quite a big ivory temple or pagoda,
kept under glass. She was nice, and gave me chocolates.
She was small, like Queen Victoria. Such thoughts are souvenirs,

they are talismans and tokens; not emotional rememberings.
These were the lives I scarcely touched, I brushed against them.
Perhaps I was aware of an atmosphere of kindness –
an old arthritic lady, in a chair, among rememberings.

NOTE   She was my mother's aunt,
my great-aunt.

30

Lovers In Pairs

Hearing the other one breathe
is a function of all paired sleepers
    and it's coupled with the wish
    such breathing should not stop.

Young lovers lay ears to hearts
and say how it would be ghastly
    if the beating faded down
    to silence – just gone away.

They think the end of the one
would be love's end, for no other
    ever would be the same.
    Of course, they're right – and wrong,

for many will come to the beds
and twenty is different from thirty,
    as sentiment's middle age
    moves slowly and coolly on.

When old ones lie side by side
what's real at last has a look-in.
    The breathing *could*, surely, stop –
    and with it the warmth of love.

It's the penultimate bed
before the one with the gravestone.
    This is what each one thinks –
    a thought sad, loving and warm.

Taking Care of the Elderly

They leave us out on the polar bear runs
so we get frozen and/or eaten

They put us outside the villages
in the jungle where the tigers pass

They choke us to death with smoke from the fires
at which they'll roast us

They put us in high-rise buildings
where the lifts don't work

They leave us to the con-men, the yobbos,
all those who rape, murder, steal

They give us inadequate, and too late, money for heating
so we die easily and slowly, of hypothermia.

Good Times

The last ten years of a life
are often a tiny bit dodgy
for Everyman and his wife –
she ends overweight and quite podgy,

though she looks after things
she does less and less of the gardening,
arthritis under the rings,
the arteries slowly hardening;

and he's not exactly handy,
slow, heavy, and jowly and paunchy –
who once was both racy and randy,
rake-thin and raffish and raunchy!

They go into the chrysalis stage,
caterpillarish appetite
shrugged off as they move through old age,
the long snooze of the day and night.

Theologians say that the soul
comes out as a butterfly next.
The Bible is there to console
and soothe all our fears with a text;

but there's no doubt that old age is sad,
mad and bad are the suitable rhymes,
and the graces that both of them had
have quite vanished like all the good times.

Sons and Mothers

There's the energy
that revs like a motorbike
vroom vroom vroom,
there's the energy
that can throw a mother
half-way across a room.
Sophisticated saloon bar sexpots
advise the cat;
but nothing except violence and violence
is going to follow that.

There's the lethargy
that spreads like a blighted fog
and covers the lot,
and the lethargy
that wants the satisfaction
they know they haven't got.
When they were little, they were affectionate
and very sweet;
but now it's nothing but violence and violence
and drugs from the street.

It's not the poor ones —
as much, or more, the rich
get high, stoned, blind
(like poor ones)
and stumble hopelessly
into that teenage ditch;
it's upper-middle mums and aristos,
not just in slums
do they have to stand for violence and violence
and land on their bums.

Joe

In a dustbin class in a dustbin school
    sits Joe;
not quite a knave and not quite a fool,
    how low
can he sink? Yes, he's on the way down,
    no job
waits for him here in this dustbin town –
    to rob,
to mug; that's what all the wild boy-gangs teach
    on streets.
For the school he's already well out of reach,
    no feats
of great teacherly skill can turn him now,
    too late
for Reading or Writing or Sacred Cow –
    the State
did its best in a land of money and graft.
    But sea
swirls round Joe, with no hope of a raft –
    no swimmer he!

A Memorial Service
in a South London Crematorium

Shall we go down South of the Border, right down, Betjeman way?
To the Cemetery in Streatham, where the mourners hope and pray?
Where the silent swift Cremation holds undisputed sway?

Down where the beefy peasants eat chips with everything?
There are sometimes Hymns on the telly, but none that they can sing –
All the worship there is vestigial, and Christ a forgotten King.

Everything's shortened to what the brain can uncomplainingly hold
And Single Syllables hold sway. The Young as well as the Old
Vaguely believe, in the woolliest way, in Eternal Cities of Gold.

Or do they? For willy-nilly this is the End of Man.
The roses on the lawn spell out their MUM, their DAD, their NAN,
As Sorrow hangs round the Departed, each Viv, each Elsie, each Stan.

It's a gesture (like a cultured pearl, the Poet's tear in the eye
Isn't *better* than the sob and the grunt or the naked animal cry)
And it recognises, in a way, that all men have to die.

Screaming Venus

If you believe the novels
(and why shouldn't you believe them?)
there are some passionate women who really let go and
scream and yell when they come –
it's as though a man were murdering a mad monkey.
And all because of continuous
lubricious friction of the bum!

I've not met it myself
(perhaps they weren't passionate women?)
or I wasn't stimulating enough to earn this tribute.
Moans there were and some sighs –
but nothing to raise the roof or annoy neighbours,
after all the strong, sinuous
delicious locking of thighs.

One girl I loved was frigid
(but this didn't make me not love her).
Ideas about sex – if they're rigid – can often be wrong too.
Pleasure, yes. Orgasm, no.
That's all she had, but very much better than nothing.
The dance was the thing, and contiguous
ambitious quick, quick, slow.

The Deaths of Poets
('Wildlife Showcase', BBC TV)

When the old honey-gathering bees
lose their strength and can no longer fly to honey
they don't walk off into the sunset like Charlie Chaplin,
brave and undaunted.

They turn their backs on the hive
and crawl away from it, the dying, unflying prey
of horrible big black spiders who paralyse them
and keep them fresh for eating.

Or they fall into the deadly path
of the black ants that swarm on them and sting them,
gangsters dedicated to the natural murder;
not sentimental.

Agincourt (1415): A Greek Epigram

Foot-soldiers and archers that starved, marched, fought.
What reward was theirs?
Pages of glory in the history books they never even saw.

In Memory of Philip Arthur Larkin, CH, OBE, 1922–1985

(Westminster Abbey, Friday, 14 February 1986)

The Church has a style, and Larkin had a style –
based on the novelist's descriptive gift
for telling detail, loading every rift
with actuality; mile after narrative mile,
he buttoned up the heat of railway carriages
with the excitement of incipient marriages,

curiously incurious, and a looker-on.
The Church isn't like that. It's keen to claim
an atheist poet who's a famous name.
He's there in Heaven, it says. For us, he's gone –
much loved, humane; that shyly gloomy humour
stays in the minds of friends, a ghost, a rumour

to those who never knew him. He looks down,
and sees at last his quite immense mistake;
Eternal Life has got him, it's no fake.
It's not a Laureate's or a Martyr's Crown,
the Order of Service says that he must suffer
this non-stop non-extinction; any duffer

must likewise live for ever. So we kneel,
though agèd stiffness makes its pained protest –
a jazz group gets some beauty off its chest,
the choir sails on, on music's even keel.
The Lesson, with archaic memorability,
is praising 'rich men furnished with ability'.

The jazz is best. Goes straight into a vein.
No hanging about, pure feeling floods the heart
with negro sadness – lost battles, from the start,
a captive people with its captive pain.
For death, no other music holds a candle
to this – even 'Lift up your hearts' by Handel!

Singing 'Abide With Me' is always fun,
though congregations seldom keep in time
and the tune wavers. A dollar to a dime
some will be late, some beat the starting gun.
More joy (memorial) would have been afforded
if they'd used poems he himself recorded,

that stuttering unstuttered genuine voice
would have made present that elusive man,
a private person, catch-me-if-you-can
and solitary; lonely, it seems, from choice.
However good professional verse-readers,
poets are best, their own more special pleaders.

'Church Going', 'An Arundel Tomb', 'Love Songs in
Age' –
sensible, conversational dying falls.
Forget the death, the death that so appals –
'a serious man on serious earth' each page
now shows him – you can cut the screams and yelling
and even organs, bidding prayers and belling –

and yet, and yet . . . an enjoyable communal act
did honour him, and certainly makes us feel
better for honouring him. A measured meal,
hieratic course by course, a sort of pact
to push the night back, belief or unbelief,
and make our death release, if not relief.

All For Love

There must be thousands of men
and in the past there must have been millions,
who have thought, 'Shall I throw it all away
and go to *her*?' Leave the wife and the kids,
though friends might use the word 'infatuated'?
Many must have thought this, but many more
hesitated.

Something has pulled them back,
out-of-the-frying-pan-into-the-fire proverbs
or just natural caution. To make love all day
for weeks on end is a thing you can't do –
it's a diseased condition, a permanent erection.
Though love and sex are powerful (and natural
selection)

you still have to live through
the long shared days, the unending breakfasts,
meet the friends who gush, who hoot, who bray,
and of course she may have children too
who might easily hate you, or be resentful.
So they settle for a life that's less exciting,
*un*eventful.

Miles Williamson-Noble

(*De Mortius*)

The Colonel didn't like him (my guess).
He called him Mr Wilkinson-Noble
(there was another officer in the unit called Wilkinson).
(Some people, of course, didn't like the Colonel.)

On bad days Miles looked like the dog Pluto.
He was rather affected and snobbish
(of me he said, 'I believe he was a commercial traveller')
(He got married and said, '*Il faut travailler pour faire l'amour!*').

When the unit was about to go overseas (1942)
his father pulled some strings, got him a home posting
(his father was a rich and successful surgeon)
(my father did quite well as a surgeon too – but he hadn't any strings).

When this happened the Battery subalterns
(egged on, I think, by the Battery Captain)
got drunk one night and poured cold water over him
as he lay asleep in bed (it was quite a cold winter).

We were in tents. I heard the screaming and cursing.
I hadn't been approached to assist this persecution
(he was my Troop Commander, I was Troop Leader)
(perhaps they felt there would be feelings of loyalty).

I didn't hate him, but I knew he was unpopular.
I remember another officer saying to me, 'A certain person
who's lying in bed with a scent-spray up his arse!'
(but he wasn't effeminate, just very superior).

My Battery Commander had said, 'That's the medical
profession for you!' (and he'd looked at me in a point-scoring way).
The funny thing was that after he was posted
we heard he'd been killed (was he bombed or something?).

The Lost Boys

An appeal comes through the letter box,
headed 'Missing O.Ws',
those with whom Wellington has lost contact,
those silly kittens who have lost their socks,
thinking perhaps, 'What's the use?'

or even, very possibly, dead.
Name of House or Dormitory, date.
Have they gone wild with Peter and Wendy?
Would the Padre say, 'They've gone ahead!'
Late for parade? Or, simply, 'late'.

Envelopes returned as 'Not known here'
or even, more foxily, 'Gone away'.
What of G. J. E. Penrose-Thackwell?
1918 is given as *his* year.
A.W.O.L., one might say.

Or P. Heber-Percy, 1922?
E. C. Richards, 1915?
willing or unwilling deserter,
missing or involved in a war or two –
school-shy or just a has-been?

NOTE   A.W.O.L. is the Army abbreviation for
'Absent Without Leave'.

Advertising Elegiacs

Advertising! The men at the front are most terribly turdlike!
    Backroom boys are the best; they can be human (a bit).
Clients are worst of the lot, bullies and thick as a blanket,
    Presentations to *them* are true purgatorial things.
Ad-managers (if they're new) want to show you that they are the
                            masters.
    Chlorophyll once was the vogue; but the Chairman's wife didn't like
                            green!
Everything greenside was out – so campaigns went out of the window.
    Thinking up replacement crap, that was the terrible bore.
That's one example, of course, but examples of this come in
                            thousands.
    This is what drives them to drink, and the heart attack bang! at the
                            end.
Suppose you've done it all once. Twice is not good. But a third time!
    Three campaigns in a row, and the brain gets a bit of a twist!
Is there a moral at all? Is there, somewhere, consolation?
    Only that death, in the end, bonks the nasties as well as the nice!

The Loved Ones

Thou hast committed –
Fornication: but that was in another country
And besides, the wench is dead.

The Jew of Malta

Men who have loved a quantity of women
go round London
from house to bar to restaurant
like Stations of the Cross,
remembering – the gain, the loss,
the once-revered addresses
of girls in summer dresses.

They run through a kind of girls'-name alphabet,
an A-Z of London,
where even the pubs remind them
of long hot love affairs . . .
who touches and who cares,
who fondles and who fancies
in these long-gone romances?

What was that all about? they are thinking
perhaps, in London –
where everything's changed and changing
in an indifferent town;
no smile, no word, no frown
from dark heads, blonde heads, red ones . . .
might just as well be dead ones.

46

Anthem

Our bones will all be built into the runway
with the bones of the Chinese coolies who are building the runway
who are starving to death and are building the runway
so that the Japanese planes may take off over the ocean.
We too shall feel faint and fall down and be built into the runway
our bones will be powdered flat with the stones and squashed into the
                                                                runway,
the bones are an indeterminate white that go into the runway,
there are no blacks or yellows or whites in the bones of the runway,
they are dry and chalky as the stones we build into the runway.
Each brings his stones and his bones for the path of the runway,
so that the Japanese planes may take off over the ocean.

Love Talk

Whatever is said,
in or on the bed
(like 'Were you
telling me a fairy story?'
or 'I want to
feel you inside me!')
is insubstantial air
circling the pubic hair . . .

From top to toe,
all the love will go
('I want to
lick you!' or 'Open
your legs a bit wider!'
or even 'I love you!'),
it will vanish away
like childhood play . . .

It stops and starts,
performing arts
(like theatre,
cinema, ballet,
there for a moment,
then slowly forgotten)
are most like this –
the insubstantial kiss . . .

Incoming Calls

They come in so happily, the incoming calls!
Stepping gaily into a room —
a room, it could be, of depression or mourning,
of someone whose sister has just died of cancer,
whose cat has been run over,
whose boyfriend or girlfriend has gone for ever . . .

The jollity of the far voices halts on the doormat,
as it were. The old friend feeling good
and wanting a long amusing chat
feels out of place, a tactless intruder.
He or she. Shut the door and stumble away — ring off —
that's all they can do.

Inspired by a Simile of Roy Fuller's

Our cars were nose to tail like sniffing dogs,
parked in adjacence at the rendezvous . . .
I thought of this while sitting in the bogs,
my mind stuck to your image then like glue –
although so many years have come and gone,
thick with events as any Irish Stew
(good with the bad, the Rebel with the Hon),
my Memory Lane still leads at times to you,
with coloured photos of the single bed –
the contacts made there once were not a few.
The lights were green before they changed to red
and everything was old, that once was new . . .

Doglike devotion, yes, that was the key.
It passed you by, but much tormented me!

High Potato Land

Every great poet in far High Potato Land
thinks he's the only true one –
total contempt for all those who don't reckon him,
homage is what must be done!

Thousands of poets in far High Potato Land –
every one thinks he's quite great –
man, woman, child, they all know they are geniuses,
that is their natural state!

There's a crime story by Highsmith that tells us of
quite a remarkable thing –
penises on the dried bodies in catacombs
shrivel to small bits of string.

This is their fear in that far High Potato Land:
big reputations may shrink.
They in their full ostentatious ubiquity
may not be great as they think!

Putney OAPs in 1985

They dribble down the High Street/ in dribs and drabs, on sticks,
the wrinkle-faced old women,/ the men with 'past it' pricks,
slow among the mums who/ wrestle with push-chair kids,
they stop for 'Hello, stranger!s'/ or 'Well, I never did!s',
clots in the pavement's bloodstream/ that bike-boys put at risk,
they wince at teenage swearing,/ tut-tutting or tsk-tsk!

When Thatcher was a nothing/ and keen on boys or horses,
they underwent the bombing,/ and the danger of the Forces.
MPs who live for money/ and the well-being of the City
don't reckon much these old ones,/ they're a bore, a drag, a pity –
not beautiful, attractive,/ fashionable or bright,
why can't they get a move on/ into that long goodnight?

They don't appear on chat shows,/ not many ask their views,
they're has-beens of the media,/ they never will be news.
So close down the old people's/ hospitals and homes
(the Welfare State, quite clearly,/ isn't loved by well-fed gnomes),
forget the War they fought in,/ way out beyond the brink –
because it *doesn't matter*/ what such old seniles think!

Sons and Lovers: Part One

The nagging wives that drive a man to drink,
the drinking men that drive a wife to nag,
the coal scuttle, the kids, the kitchen sink,
the pregnancies that make her belly sag,
the little houses packed in, back to back,
like the poor sleeping husband and poor wife –
for those with work, a smoking chimney stack,
others stay cold, an unrewarding life
though neighbours with coarse kindness bring some help,
it's still an animal thing, like dog and bitch,
fawn to the masters, snarl, suckle and whelp,
make do and mend, clean, cook, and knit or stitch –

till Saturday's beer breaks in, hot cock and hen,
the night that starts the cycle going again.

'A Piece of Cake'
(In Memoriam Dieppe, 19 August 1942)

No, the murders left no traces on the shore,
no, the murders left no traces
on the bright and murdered places
where the murderers were active once before,

and the sun shines bright on that bright promenade
where the slayers crouched to slay them,
there was massacre and mayhem —
because, to tell the truth, it isn't hard

(though there are hundreds in the landing craft)
if you know you'll be invaded
and you have them enfiladed,
to mow them down at leisure, fore and aft.

Just the accidental skirmish out at sea
and they went to Action Stations.
All they needed then was patience,
like the spider in his web — you must agree

it wasn't hard, with strong points on the cliffs,
you could do it sitting, standing,
even though the tanks were landing
you could knock them out without the 'buts' and 'ifs'.

No, the murders left no traces on this scene;
where there once were blown-up bodies
kids with eyes like silly Noddy's
run in joy as though that war had never been.

Dieppe, August 1984

NOTE   The Dieppe Raid of 1942 had as its centrepiece a
frontal attack on the town by Canadian troops, towed across
the Channel in landing craft. The operation was comprom-

ised, not by any security leaks, but because a German E-boat patrol sighted the left flank of the convoy and opened fire. If communications had been better, the raid might have been called off, even at this late stage. The whole operation depended on very exact timing (waves of fighters attacking the town) and the timing went wrong. One battleship shelling the defences would have made a lot of difference, but the Royal Navy reserved its battleships for the Atlantic War. As a result, the Canadians lost 56 officers and 851 other ranks. One Army officer at the briefing is supposed to have told the regimental commanders that the raid would be 'a piece of cake'.

All Souls

This is the room where the great poet breathed his last.
His breathtaking originality is now like mist on the air.
Here is the desk where he worked, and in the corner
is the old wind-up gramophone that helped him when he typed.

There are photos of friends, and letters: *Cher collègue*!
In glass-fronted bookcases are his books, including his
Collected Poems translated into Icelandic.

In the master-bedroom there are photographs of his wife.
She has less of an aura, but nonetheless she is there.
He is the star, the children are photo-appendages, like the small
groups, quite informal, of him with the great Other Writers.
He didn't have much taste in pictures, the landscapes are dullish.
To show honesty, perhaps to shock, is a detailed line-drawing
of the small obstinate penis that caused him so much trouble.

Some love-letters survive, with the work-sheets of verse.
There are even, like sleeping beauties, curled locks of their hair.

The There Then meets the Here Now in piped appropriate
music, its fixed harmonies run like lost dogs through the rooms.
His walking stick too lies doglike in a glass case.
It will never walk again, 'it has finished with walking',
as his pupil expressed it in the famous memorial poem.

Going into the Details

There are scholars who
get hooked on all the particulars
in Dictionaries of Slang,
e.g. 'to fist it (of a woman):
to seize the *membrum virile*
with a sexual intention'.
There are many others I could mention.

Even though it's all
stigmatised as 'low', 'colloquial'
and obsolete as well,
the learnèd lovers really like it
(though, indeed, the whole language,
one could say, is obsolescent).
Such words make a don or two tumescent.

But this is to put
a magnifying glass on every letter,
the language of love
takes in much baboon behaviour,
you don't need reams of Latin
to get the actual satisfaction.
Idiots too are in the web of thought and action.

Jurisdiction

I want to be a Hittite Priest-King
but the Canadian Geese on the lake are barking like dogs
and over them I have no jurisdiction.

I am warm, I am comfortable, I am staying in a guest-room
where Yeats once stayed in the 1920s.
It's a high-class guest-room and a charming duplex,

by the main entrance and covered with ivy,
nicknamed by the College simply 'The Prophet's Chamber',
where the Bible-bashing preachers relaxed from their labours

in the days when Divines were the reverend visitors –
and far more than me like the Hittite Priest-Kings.
But the geese on the lake still escaped their jurisdiction.

Wells College, Aurora, N.Y.,
April 1986

Part Two
The So-Called Sonnets

'I Didn't Have Enough Sex'

(John Betjeman in old age)

In my bad dream I paid the man in the caff.
Threepence for the tea. Then moved away.
I drank half, then came back for some sugar.
'I know your sort!' he said (or something such).
He poured my cup of tea into the sink.
'I paid for that!' I said. But he just looked,
confident, arrogant, a kind of god.
He gave no answer but a settled hate.

Dreams in which we are slighted and disliked.
And never get the things we ought to have.
Think of the millions! Betjeman's Complaint!
The beautiful, the young, the commercial sellers
are rare exceptions (and they have too much).
The sugar and the god are usual.

British Poets

We don't get jailed for criticising the Government,
or sent into exile or into lunatic asylums,
the small freezing concrete cells are not for us.
Even the avant-garde lives in bourgeois comfort,
in Polys and suchlike, teaching – part of the Establishment.
Hard labour, sleeping on sacks, the whips, the dogs,
we live apart from these, in limited envy.
We can even manage humour, and not always bitter.

It's really only in Northern Ireland the cracks are showing
(what you might call an Arab-Israeli situation);
three hundred years earlier the men were planted
like dragon's teeth. So now we have cowardly heroes
and a chance to write of political suffering,
like the genuine Russian, European, South African sufferers!

The Daytime Mugging in the High Street

Who would want to attack that poor little thing
Walking up Putney High Street at 9.30 in the morning,
without a thought in her head except to get to Putney BR Station
and then to Clapham Junction, to a sale at Arding & Hobbs,
with a view to buying a quilt, or was it a fan-heater?
Well, somebody did! Went for her purse in her basket,
pushed her into the road. Severe bruising, three lower vertebrae
cracked.
A young chap, he missed the purse, made off into Fulham.

I reckon he was a loony; or an addict, crazy on a Monday morning,
needing a fix after the weekend. Who knows? She didn't even see him.
Luckily for her, there wasn't any traffic. Thrown into a main road,
she could have been killed. All the conventional judgments
say what a terrible thing (true) and what a terrible man!
But I say, too, she *might* still be better off than a tormented young
junkie.

Protein

I can confidently predict that very soon we shall all be dead.
On the telly a horrible white mantis, looking far too much
like something out of a ghost story by M. R. James,
has caught a great big beautiful Brazilian butterfly.
Fairly slowly, as it clasps it, it begins to eat its head.
The wings still flap pathetically. Oh, yes, we wince.

But our horror is not pure, it's two-way sympathy.
We feel those wings beating in our own mouths, we're so omnivorous.
After all, dogs (beloved dogs) eat baby rabbits head first
and I expect cats do too (they certainly eat baby rabbits).
We do nasty things to calves and battery hens
and quite disgusting things to geese in Strasbourg.
You just have to get your protein from something.
Like the Army living rough, eating worms – also on telly.

The Garrotting
('It's an Old Spanish Custom')

In an Exhibition devoted to the Art of Barcelona
there is this picture of a public execution –
I marvel at the date – 1894!
But no, it's in modern dress, a crowd in a big square,
the seated victim, the hypocrites crowding round,
telling him Jesus loves him as the iron collar tightens,
the executioner turns the screw that's boring in
below the skull, to kill the spinal cord.
Are the men in pointed hats the Inquisition?
This is Old Spanish Cruelty. The suffering
benefits sadists only, a threat, something to show
that *status quo* has meaning in the world.

I think of Larkin's hard throat cancer death,
better than being garrotted – but not much.

February 1986

NOTE   The last public execution in Britain took place in
1866.

Making Love to Women

Auden said making love to women was 'too easy'.
I and another old man (both, you could say, lovers of women)
consider this statement. With laughter.
Those who don't care or who don't take it seriously
are not affected by anxiety – both Auden and Isherwood,
without any doubt they could go through the motions.
It meant nothing to them. Now with *boys* it was different –
here the love was less 'easy', there was infatuation.

Do lesbians think making love to a man is 'too easy'?
I've never heard so. But, with Yeats,
'the fascination of what's difficult'
was a potent factor; and surely all such questions
are fraught with interest? Auden also said the 'fucking'
was the most disagreeable part of an affair.

NOTE   See p. 368 of Stephen Spender's *Journals 1939–1983*.
Auden is supposed to have said to Margaret Gardiner in 1929,
'What I hate is the fucking.'

Intermittent Claudication

I told a doctor, at a party, all about how
I kicked a football in a dream and next day
my left knee was strained and extremely painful
and how I walked about 5½ miles to a bookshop in Toronto
and the calf of my left leg gave up.
It comes and goes, I said.

What you have, an effect of old age, he said,
is called intermittent claudication.
You remember the lameness of the Emperor Claudius?

But what I remembered was the medical report on Yeats:
We have here an agèd arteriosclerotic (was his doctor Gogarty?)
and how Yeats said he would rather be called an agèd arteriosclerotic
than King of Lower Egypt.

Ah, the words! The words! They can reconcile us to anything!

NOTE   The name of Claudius has nothing to do with lameness.
Claudicare (= to limp) and *Claudicatio* (= limping) are both
straightforward Latin, and favourite words of Cicero's.

Into Science Fiction

When you find yourself in a spacetram
with a big tough feminid called Tnuc,
who is having it off with a small delicate feminid
called Sirotilc – on a planet called Odlid –
and there are two terrible entities called Zbog
and Vrig, and all the names of the humanoids
are anagrams or palindromes or unpronounceable . . .
why, then you'll know you're into Science Fiction.

Which hasn't moved since Mr Nosnibor and Erewhon –
although the Aliens have taken over Algolagnia
since the Time Traveller set out, since the Eloi and the Morlocks,
and Einstein has freaked out with the bug-eyed monsters.
The theories, the technologies, are sexed as adventure stories
suitable for green teenagers with nine purple arms . . .

Psychiatrist, Heal Thyself!

Once the husband of my sister who died
nearly twenty years ago. Then Consultant
in this very hospital where he is now,
the biggest loony bin in the South-West;
Sir Arthur Quiller-Couch's daughter Fowey,
they say, a fellow-patient.
Healthy and happy, but the mind has gone,
the memory doesn't really work.

Does he know *me*? It's hard to say. He doesn't
call me Gavin. He seriously says,
'I don't go to London much these days.'
All questions are asked two, three, four times.

On the wall in the ward, for these casualties, is a notice:
YOU ARE IN ST LAWRENCE HOSPITAL, BODMIN, CORNWALL.

Part Three

Shall I Die?

(A Critical Exercise)

Did the Bard try quite hard
when he wrote what they quote –
               a new-found poem?
It is good? or dead wood?
Starched and stiff? Who knows if
               scholars know 'em,
the true joys, Real McCoys,
and worthy of Shakespeare's great canon?
               They attribute; he is mute.
So easily it might be by Anon!

Where the words fly like birds
some young ponce thinks they're nonce,
               while others, snarling,
say the Muse would refuse
to undress – it's a mess –
               or be Will's darling!
Suspicious doubt, O keep out!
The rooms in God's famous huge mansion
               aren't reserved, nor yet deserved
by dabblers in dubious scansion!

The rights and wrongs of Shaker's songs!
He's so posh – but they're tosh
               in several places.
Any fool, who's *not* choir school,
as you know, sings high and low –
               your true love's graces
aren't much praised when this is raised
as sign of remarkable merit!
               You don't remark 'Oh, hark!'
when rabbits squeal loud at a ferret.

Dons explain 'wind and rain' –
but *you* try 'When that I
                was and a little
tiny boy'! Grammar's joy
it is *not*, nor so hot!
                No jot or tittle!
It *does* prove songs that move
rely on the music, and singing –
                smooth nonsense can unnerve a man.
junk food can set dinner bells ringing!

        'Cheeks', 'brows', 'hair', 'beyond compare',
        and a 'dove'? Words of love
                frequent such lyrics.
        Not just Will! Bad writers still
        use them all, though talent's small,
                in panegyrics.
        Faded now – but, somehow,
in earlier days they were voguish.
        Georgian Verse could immerse
a sex urge in terms then thought roguish.

        It's bad enough, it's awful stuff;
        by him, when young, what might be *sung*
                did get written.
        But stand aloof (there's no proof),
        you must chew words that you
                too fast have bitten!
        And cheeks, instead of lips, are red!
While noses, like foreheads, can wrinkle!
        And sure as eggs, from our legs
comes an unmistakable tinkle!

NOTE   The poem 'Shall I die?' included in the 'Bodleian MS Rawl poet 160' (its jovial nickname among scholars) was attributed to Shakespeare in or around 1630. Later commentators have not agreed. Malone, for example, the great 18th-century Shakespeare editor, seems not to have supported the attribution. Mr Gary Taylor, using computer analysis of the vocabulary, now claims that neologisms and parallels with existing work known to be by Shakespeare make it likely that the attribution is correct. One reason for doubting this, it has been pointed out, is the fact that love songs of c. 1600 all share the same vocabulary (the vocabulary, roughly, derided in Shakespeare's famous Sonnet 130 – 'My mistress' eyes are nothing like the sun'). The line 'Suspicious doubt, O keep out!', in my second stanza, occurs in the original poem.

The Madness of a Headmistress

Don't be a fool, don't go to school,
don't put a foot outside –
Old Miss Oysterley
is eating bubblegum,
Sellotape, tin-tacks and Tide!

Be like a mouse, stay in the house –
her mouth is open wide –
weird Miss Oysterley
is drinking printer's ink,
paint and insecticide!

Don't go near the Head, just stay in bed –
jump in a box and hide –
Old Miss Oysterley
is fond of the little ones,
roasted or frittered or fried!

It's very sad, she's gone quite mad,
her brain is quite putrefied –
poor Miss Oysterley
munching through Infants I
that once was her joy and her pride!

The Poets' Revolt

In *Poetry Review* (Volume 75, Number 4) there is a League
Table of the living British and Irish poets, divided into four
Divisions, as in the Football League. The list begins with all the
H's – Heaney, Hughes, Hill, Harrison (in that order). This is
the work of John Sheeran, of Oxford University. Altogether, 92
poets are 'placed'.

Heaney is the only one
who'll be pleased with what he's done –
you can't say the same for Hughes,
Laureates hate being Number 2s.
You don't need a Holmes or Freud
to guess they'll *all* be quite annoyed
to see that they've been ranked below
frauds and pseuds like So-and-So.
Kit Wright numbered 89 –
put down so far he's in a mine!
One First Division woman (20) –
one woman only, and that's plenty –
that seems to be the general gist
of this dreaded donlike list.
And Wendy Cope at 91!

Surely it would be quite fun
(and poets, surely, should be able)
to make a *Critical* League Table
where all the dons who love to spout
and splash like whales and swim about
had numbers stuck upon their backs.
All open to harpoon attacks.
Guess who'd be bottom! Just guess who!
Sheeran! Like Patten (92)!

Vicar's Daughter Raped by Fiend

(Headline, the *Sun*, 7 March 1986)

Who but a Fiend would rape a Vicar's daughter?
So deaf to all appeals to Christian charity,
So blind to Love and Lust – their vast disparity –
So hot from Hell, so breathing fire and slaughter!
No need to reason or to seek out proof,
Plain as the saintliness of Saint Theresa,
He was no likely lad, she no cock-teaser,
He had the horn, he had the cloven hoof!

She was an Angel – that's quite likely too –
Folklore runs deep in every yellow press –
Each tabloid Born-Again from day to day
Loves anything that's blasphemous *and* blue,
Her shapely tits escaping from a dress
Over their minds quite obviously hold sway!

Re-assessing Modern Masters

At first they say, 'He's very wonderful!'
then they say, 'He's very wonderful but . . .'
Just a bit old-fashioned they may not say – but think.
'When he wrote that he must have been half-cut!'
'His anti-sexist immune defence system*
must have been on the blink!'

'Of course he was remarkable in his lifetime –
but we've moved on from there.'
They think his preoccupations very old hat,
like outdated slang or poems on lips or hair.
They cut no ice with them. Or melt, or soften,
each frozen critical cat!

* Compare Acquired Immune Deficiency Syndrome

Sonnet 155

(Never Before Imprinted)

I stand as doubtful in the eye of Time,
The day unknown that fairly gave me birth,
Obscure I am and in obscurer rhyme
I hid myself, my woe, my youthful mirth,
My rustic marriage to uncertain Anne,
The years in that great city where the play
Seduced my honeyed Muse, where I began
To harvest in my wit, in the world's way.
I hid my loves, though players did report
Encounters in the deep deceitful dark,
While some were wont to say I loved the Court,
Sweet ladies deer in that high scented park.
 My life I am content should be unknown,
 So that my works to Time shall still be shown.

NOTE Shakespeare's actual day of birth remains a matter of conjecture. The details of his marriage to Anne Hathaway, at the age of 18, are confused. Nothing is known of his early life in London. Contemporaries reported both that he was indifferent to Court approbation, and that he was at ease there and welcomed it. The 'dark lady' of the Sonnets is still not certainly identified. Apart from signatures on documents, no specimen of Shakespeare's 'honied muse' was referred to by a contemporary.

'Sex in the Soapsuds'

(Found poem, *Wandsworth & Putney Guardian*, 30 January 1986)

Romping Romeos indulge in steamy launderette love-ins
while their dirty linen is washing.
As their clothes tumble in the dryer
they tumble sexily in the soapsuds.
And their lust is getting launderette owners in a lather.
This is just one of the vices soiling
the whiter-than-white image of our launderettes.
Laundry staff allege that customers
have sex in front of washing machines
sniff glue and smoke pot
beat up staff
intimidate managers
spit on old ladies' clean undies . . .

Mavie Nolan, who works at the Coin-op, Bedford Hill,
says she can hardly believe
how people abuse her launderette.
'I come in and a couple are having sex.'

Cause and Effect

Wives of drinking husbands
never stop to think
that it's anti-drinking nagging
that drives them all to drink.

A Kilkenny Cat
(The Power of Magic)

Walking up the hill past the Castle
on a cold late November morning –
on the frosted wood of a bench,
with a woolly-gloved finger,
I make the Sign of the Cunt,
a crude drawn outline . . .

Farther up the hill I meet, walking down,
a very pretty girl. She smiles
and says *Good morning*! (unaccosted by me).

Surely that Sign was auspicious!
Kilkenny 28 November 1985
Putney 23 February 1986

Hell in Putney

(mostly found, *Wandsworth & Putney Guardian*, 30 May 1985)

There's just a little too much billing and cooing
around Sarah House, Arabella Drive!
Tenant Mrs Ruby Hattersley said:
'The entrance to the flats is diabolical.'
Any minute they're expecting
the Pigeon Prince of Darkness to arrive!

The council put up netting to stop them roosting –
'There's pigeon mess,' said Mrs Hattersley, 'everywhere!
They go in behind the netting and it stops them falling off.
They love it!' Those stains are biological!
Housing Management Chairman Peter Bingle
is really tearing out his hair!

'For every bird we trap,' he's quoted as saying,
'there seems to be two or three to replace them.
I just wish this was a problem that would fly away!'
Is the answer perhaps carbolical?
'It is really giving us the bird!' says Peter.
The problems of Evil in Putney – we must face them!

Lewis Carroll's Health Rules

If you have a cold
you must eat a lot of crumpets
and blow your nose like trumpets
and do as you are told.

If you have a cough
you must drink a lot of Guinness
and drive about in Minis
and try to have it off.

If you have a corn
you must boil your feet in syrup,
teach budgies how to chirrup,
and practise the French Horn.

If you're down with flu
you must ride around on piglets
and eat mince-pies and Twiglets
till everything turns blue.

If you have a sprain
you must wrap it round with raffia,
and call Sicilian Mafia
to give you some real pain.

A Jig for John F. Deane
and *Poetry Ireland*

The fine City of Dublin!
With joy we're all bubblin,
no toilin and troublin,
   it's there in the sun,
so happy and glorious
(the cold wind is Boreas) –
and the Emperor's Warriors*
   add to the fun!

And no Victor or Valerie
needs a great salary,
the National Gallery
   opens its doors!
No pamphlet or fascicle
can beat Neo-Classical –
whose scenes lad-and-lassical
   Poussin encores!

Our hearts go all fluttery,
prayerful and muttery –
like boys in the buttery
   sinkin their jars
we look up imploringly,
gladly, adoringly,
as Great Art unboringly
   wings to the stars!

Three-person'd God's battery
flames above flattery,
a Sligo-born Slattery
    thrills to the paint!
The Four Courts are flamin
with sun, it's quite shamin –
their beauty I'm blamin,
    I'm feelin quite faint!

O Eireann Eire,
my secretest sharer,
your Dublin shines clearer
    than Fastnet sea-fog –
or rains of the Amazon.
My headache hammers on,
bring me some Jameson,
    the hair of the dog!

* An Exhibition of an early Chinese Emperor's
guardian statues at the Royal Hospital
in Kilmainham.

Sally

'Are you interested in knowing when and whom you will marry? What
the year will bring you? If you will gain in a lawsuit? . . . What are
you best adapted for? If you have enemies and who? If you can trust
your friends? Why your love acts strange? What lies in the future
and what fate awaits you?'

New York street handout

Anglo-Saxon Sally operates between Third and Lexington –
she makes large claims:
'Forecasts – Future – Past – Present
with Palm, Tarot Cards, Crystal Ball, Readings.
Are her clients all dames?

Or does the SPECIAL WITH THIS AD Regular Card Reading
$5.00 OFF
offered to the street-passers
pull in young, confused, gullible, male New Yorkers,
chauvinist at the pig-trough?

Tune in to these thoughts: 'Why don't that Marylene let me
touch up her ass?'
'Why she act so strange, man?'
It doesn't seem likely, probable – or possible even.
No, a different class,

the unsure more-than-mature woman is here targeted.
'That Mrs Feinblatt,
she look at me in a funny way!'
'Ed don't love me any more. He think I'm done for, past it!'
'Mr Fink's a dirty rat.'

Or just a bit younger? When Romance can be mentioned,
Love that will last.
'Will Wilbur ever kiss me?'
Sally knows these thoughts like the colour of the dollars,
forecasting the Past.

New York, June 1985

The Damsel-Fly

'The yin that did it last time,
A canna dae it noo!'
The Ball of Kirriemuir

The damsel-fly
is a pretty spry
small kind of dragon-fly,
in every way it is pretty fly.

When the male makes love
it doesn't need Martinis –
and it has a very remarkable penis.

It doesn't read Sex Manuals
or, indeed, *any* books –
but its prominent pintle is furnished with hooks.

With these it hooks out the sperm
left behind by any previous lover –
and substitutes its own. It's a real undercover

secret agent in the
miraculous Courts of Love . . .
Venus ought to promote the damsel-fly.
It's far cleverer than the dove!

Tallness is All

Pope and Keats were nothings,
only two feet high –
all the enormous Sitwells
were towering to the sky.

Edith once told Bottrall
physical size was all –
miniature masterpieces weren't on,
by anybody small!

All long, or little, poems
by Thwaite or Taner Baybars
are bound to be a waste of time
and, you might say, lost labours.

No chance for midget madrigals –
the Muse abhors dwarf dwellings.
The palaces of giants alone,
with music's sweetest swellings,

grotesque and slightly clumsy,
but *large* and madly airy,
are where she likes to take her ease,
a fatuous fat fairy.

So little people, leprechauns,
and those the size of Japs,
need not apply as geniuses –
the fitting of the caps

goes on, and Immortality
(despising sound and sense)
will only settle on your head
if you are quite immense!

NOTE   Keats was in fact 5 ft 2 in tall, and Pope 4 ft 6 in.

Behaviour Unbecoming a Lady
in a British Cultural Centre

At the Poetry Society
there were men of notoriety
saying farewell to all anxiety
and their usual sobriety –
        they had had an awful lot.
As they plunged into the liquor,
as their brains began to flicker,
they got much much drunker quicker,
        gave it all they'd got!

Yes, they needed all their talents
to maintain a state of balance –
full like mainsails and top-gallants,
they were quite uncanny callants;
        fou as any fiery Scot!
A birthday was being celebrated –
with booze bottled, canned and crated –
to stop *him* being underrated,
        like Lang Syne forgot!

Unsober night of worthy cotter
(not some starchy English rotter)!
They soaked drink like any blotter,
they could barely stand or totter
        like an infant from his cot!
Poets, yes, but also boozers –
beggars (buggers) can't be choosers,
whisky-winners, lager-losers,
        each distinguished sot!

Watching them, a poetette.
She could not play hard to get,
between her legs she might be wet –
but not behind the ears, you bet!
    For all *men* she was quite hot.
Other girls might think a lady'd
not make women so degraded –
she, for males both fresh and faded,
    had her softest spot.

She, as well, had not absented
self (or lips) from what's fermented,
till her self-control was dented –
the gayness was what *she* resented.
    So there, at once, to stop the rot,
she incontinently decided
to follow where her instincts guided!
Some have foolishly derided,
    as black kettle pot,

all that's gay, each satisfaction
stemming from same-sex attraction,
all the homosexual faction –
she preferred to take some action!
    Cowardly, oh, she was not!
Towards them she at once proceeded,
grabbed their private parts and kneaded
(it was quite *outré*, dear, what she did),
    so to frig and frot

those so gentlemanly members!
Did she hope to stir some embers
of what Adam still remembers –
Eve's hot sun in our Decembers?
    Like a sexy sans-culotte!
Envy? She could not enjoy them.
Probably just to annoy them.
They, for her, would not employ them.
    So, they were a blot

on the landscape of her thinking –
she, remember, had been drinking,
with her Super-ego shrinking,
in womanly confusion sinking
    many a stirring tot and shot.
Not one rose up like an airman
to stand up primitive, a bare man!
Instead, complaints went to the Chairman!
    That's what!

A Wee Laberlethin
For the Lads Wi' the Lallans
(See *The Concise Scots Dictionary*, 1985)

Och, lackanee! alas! an' wae!
The Muse o' birse-cups an' the brae,
yon lammie-meh ye cuddle tae,
    she's aiblins left ye
an' o' the sense tae sing or say
    she's sure bereft ye!

D'ye no mind John Logie Baird,
wha rules the soun' waves lek a laird,
wha blins the sicht till nane are spared,
    an' fettles baith –
gars mak a lame, a mant, a *merde*
    wi' laidron laith?

Ye lawbour on your lawboards still,
but Telly taps Parnassus Hill,
ye hae the bensell an' the will
    but still ye're waitin'
the Muse – an' she'll be missin' till
    ye write i' Laitin!

Lacklustre labsters! Lampeekoo
is a' ye're fit for here an' noo,
lawins an' lounrie when ye're fou,
    lampin' alang
wi' sic lamgabblich – as a coo
    might mak a sang!

Ye'll not owercome the pow'r o' Ringo,
or a' the glamourie o' Bingo,
or Sex, flumgummery flamingo –
    high-kiltit verse
will aye be in their lugs laich lingo
    an' Fame's reverse!

94

Ye laik, ye laig, ye lauch, ye lagger,
ye claut the laggin till ye stagger –
lak lacrissye they laib Mick Jagger,
    your lays stir anger,
lang lugs, ye slay lek dirk or dagger
    wi' fearfu' langour!

Knapdarlocks, in your kneggum strang,
fa' silent, ye hae sung owerlang
the Scots your kickmaleeries wrang!
    Leave th' kilfuddoch!
Ye've nae mair aptitude for sang
    than th' puir puddock!

GLOSSARY

laberlethin a rigmarole, rambling discourse (la 19th-20thC)
lackance alas (la 19thC)
birse-cup final cup of tea with whisky instead of milk (e20thC)
lammie-meh pet name for a lamb (20thC)
fettle go for (a person) (la 19thC)
lame a critical injury (15-e16thC)
mant a stutter, a stammer (19thC)
laidron rascal, loafer (16thC)
laith evil (la 14th-15thC)
lawbour = labour
lawboard (*Labrod*) lapboard, a board laid across the knees for
    working on (19th-e20thC)
bensell force, violence (la 17th-e20thC)
lampeekoo a variation of hide-and-seek
lawins a session of drinking, esp. in a tavern (16th-17thC)
lounrie sexual wickedness, fornication (la 16th-e18thC)
lamp stride along (17thC)
lamgabblich a long rambling discourse, a rigmarole (20thC)
glamourie = glamour (18C-e20thC)
flumgummery any foolish or frivolous thing
high-kiltit having the skirts well tucked up, immodest, indecent (la
    18th-e20thC)
laich low (la 14thC)
laik amuse oneself (15th-16thC)

laig chatter (la 19thC)
lauch laugh (la 14th C)
lagger sink in mud or soft ground (18thC)
claut the laggin drain a container of drink (la 18th-19thC)
lacrissye liquorice (la 15th-16thC)
laib lick up, lap, gobble (18thC)
lang lugs a donkey (a person with long ears) (18thC)
langour boredom (la 15thC)
knapdarlock hardened dirt or dung hanging from the tail of an
    animal, a dirty, cheeky person (1. la 19thC, 2.20thC)
kneggum disagreeable taste or flavour (la 18thC)
kickmaleerie a flimsy trifling thing (19thC)
kilfuddoch a meeting and discussion (19thC)
puddock a toad (or frog) (la 16thC)

Breakfast All Day

(Notice outside a café in the Lower Richmond Road)

Breakfast all day!
What a marvellous thought!

Fresh orange juice, cereals,
eggs and bacon, toast, marmalade,
tea or coffee!
Or even pancakes and maple syrup,
buckwheat cakes, bagels, iced water!

In Heaven I bet they have
breakfast all day –
with Room Service angels –
and the taste and the joy and the appetite
stay fresh, all day!

Unhappiness Begins at Home

Horace once wrote a poem
saying that high feelings are all very well
but the most serious thing for a poet
is to have a cold.

4,000 people die in an earthquake
in Mexico City;
an old lady in her seventies
(close friend of my old dead aunt)
is told she must have a foot amputated.

But all I worry about
is that I have only one poem
in a new anthology of representative verse.

Small Ads

On the back page of a Sunday paper
are the Small Ads and the Crossword and all that caper:

'NEW AUTHORS! Tired of rejection?'
'Not vanity publishing!' (This is the *literary* section.)

'All categories considered including
war memoirs, autobiographies and poetry.' Also, the self-deluding.

Between ATTACK CANCER and TIES NARROWED
these narrow roads to Fame are modestly and tastefully arrowed.

So are NEXUS, SELECT FRIENDS, UNATTACHED?
Somewhere there's somebody with whom you might be discreetly
matched

there's no mention of orgies or binges.
Just LATEX RUBBERWEAR, VASECTOMY, and ENEMA
SYRINGES.

Nothing to excite lust or loathing –
unless you're turned on by EXPECTATIONS ('leather and rubber
clothing'

Do GAY LINK INTROS hint seductions?
It says 'discretion assured'. 'Nationwide male and female gay
introductions

It's all a bit shadowy, what these proffer –
but there's nothing one bit shadowy about the DUREX FREE
OFFEI

Names named. Prices. Take a siesta –
lie down and dream of FETHERLITE, NUFORM, BLACK
SHADOW, FIEST/

This is *it* for SELECT FRIENDS you dated,
quite bowled over by the charms of your GOSSAMER
                                          LUBRICATED!

And there's something rich and strange
about the missile-worthy names of the celebrated AEGIS RANGE:

STIMULANT OR DELAY. What joy!
ROUGH OR RIBBED, FRUIT FLAVOURED, TIGHT FIT,
                                          BIG BOY!

High heels! Underwear! You won't look back
once you get stuck into that extra special SUPER VARIETY
                                          SELECTION PACK!

100

Kingsley Has a Go at a Latin Poem

Stabat mulier beata,
omnibus conspicua, mammeata,
invidia multis iam conflata!

Praeclara tamen stat papilla,
odor fragrans in axilla,
meretrix, nomine Camilla!

Centuriones sunt amentes,
Venus flagellat omnes gentes,
cupidines non sunt absentes.

Magnitudo erectionum
optimum eis certe bonum,
plaudunt, magnum faciunt sonum.

Miraculum labia maiora
sed autem, quae sunt meliora,
dulcissima labia minora!

Amantium precationes
et ejaculationes
longae sicut orationes!

Languescunt, partem femineam
illae Camillae pensant ream.
Laudunt omnes illam deam!

Translation A happy woman was standing, in the sight of all,
big-breasted, the envy of many straightway excited! Very beauti-
ful, in the same way, stands out the nipple, there is a fragrant
odour in the armpit – she is a harlot, by name Camilla! The
centurions are out of their minds, Venus lashes all the nations,
desires are not absent. The size of their erections is to them, for
certain, of the highest good, they applaud, they make a great noise.

A wonder to see her labia majora – but moreover, what are even better, her very sweet labia minora! The prayers of her lovers, and their ejaculations, are as long as public speeches! They faint with languor, they consider the womanly part of that Camilla to be the cause. All praise that goddess!

NOTE   The Rev. Charles Kingsley, best known as the author of *The Water Babies*, *Westward Ho!* and a handful of poems, was remarkable for his belief that life in Heaven consisted of never-ending sexual inter-course – a belief not common in his lifetime (1819–1875). His model here is the rhymed poem in Latin written by monks in the Middle Ages, usually a hymn.

My Life in the Theatre

In 1933 I played the part of a Student
(in Greek) in Aristophanes' *Clouds* at Wellington.

In 1937 I wrote the words of a song
that was performed by the Footlights at Cambridge.

In the same year (I think) I scene-shifted *The Queen of Spades*
and fell (accidentally) into the arms of Pat Rawdon-Smith.

In 1979 my words to John Gardner's *Tobermory*
were sung at three performances – Royal Academy of Music.

Of the Poetry Readings in theatres
we do not wish to speak.

Rubaiyat of the Prostate

Awake! For in the Lavatory Bowls of Night
Old Men have peed and stained the brilliant White:
    And Lo! the Yellowness of Age has dimmed
The Star of Youth that once shone bold and bright!

Ah, me, once Damsels all they had bestowed
On those Young Men who batted, bowled and rowed –
    Though they to all and sundry, on their Bikes,
Their rosy Knickers in the Daylight showed!

'Tis at this age that we remember How –
But no more have we, Friends, the Strength; enow
    To lay the Loved Ones in the silken Bed!
Though HE did us so mightily endow!

Strange, is it not? That Sailors, greatly thewed,
By us with Godlike Beauty were imbued:
    And now from Sea return'd lie still in Earth,
That erst so dazzled us, when in the Nude!

The Wine, the Grape, the Visions that we saw –
And shared, it seemeth, with great Evelyn Waugh!
    Ah, these the Liver faintly doth forbid.
Once Nightingales, but now the black Rook's Caw!

I dreamed that Dawn's Left Hand was in my Fly
And lighted was the Candle, burning high!
    But, waking, saw with disappointed Gaze
That Light a flicker, and about to die.

The Roses and the Gardens, let them go!
Our Youth, our Love, that we once fancied so,
   Forget them, as the Nights of Too Much Wine
Blot out all Memory like falling Snow!

NOTES   'Dawn's Left Hand' is a phrase that actually
occurs in Fitzgerald's masterpiece. He had a very idealised
love for sailors. The *Ruba`i* is a Persian quatrain (rhyming as
above), used by Omar Khayyam in the 12th century.

The Kidnapping of the Lindbergh Baby
(1932)

What a country for crime!
American criminals are the best!
Just look what these simple kidnappers achieved:
they took the child from a house full of people,
they collected a large ransom,
they escaped all consequences,
the wrong man was executed for the crime,
and lastly (not that it mattered to them)
they killed the baby.

Kipper

(Rudyard Kipling died in 1936)

I went out to a Salong – they invited me an' all –
An' a bloke in fancy dress, 'e looked down at me, so tall;
An' 'e wouldn't tike me ulster, nor 'e wouldn't tike me'at.
'Presoomably,' 'e says, says 'e, 'You're *known* to Mrs Catt?'
    Ow! It's Kipper this, an' Kipper that, an' 'Wot a little runt!'
    But I'll 'ave me revenge indeed when blue-blood boys wot 'unt
    Mikes me out their bloomin' mascot! Yes, the idiots wot 'unt
    Won't think me such a runt no more – them blue-blood boys wot
                                   'unt!

I 'eard the screamin' cows that sing (if singin's wot they do);
To me it sounds uncommon like they're bustin' for the loo!
There was funny pictures on the wall, an' a woman stiff as tin
She says to me, all ladylike, 'Why, 'ow did *you* get in?'
    Ow! It's Kipper this, an' Kipper that, an' 'Go back to Stone'enge!'
    But I'm a Primal Tory an' I *will* 'ave me revenge,
    I'm a blasted Ancient Briton, an' I'll tike me own revenge –
    With the 'elp o' them Young Fogies I shall tike me own revenge!

Intellectuals an' reds that reads me books turns pile!
I'm especially vindictive in that Mary Postgate tile!
I'm a bully that was bullied (see the evidence in print),
You'd best keep clear o' me, me boys, if you can tike an 'int!
    Ow! It's Kipper this an' Kipper that, an' ''E's a Philistine!'
    But I'm full o' that Hinitiative an' I knows well wot is mine,
    Yes, I knows well wot is mine, me boys, I knows full well wot's mine,
    I'm Private Enterprise 'isself, true blue, I knows wot's mine!

No, I'm not no blinkin' blossom sich as you might see at Kew,
I 'ates the rich an' idle, I'm suspicious o' the Jew –
I loves Hindians an' Irish *but* (an' 'ere's a funny thing)
I only loves 'em when they fights for me own Queen or King!
    Ow! It's Kipper this an' Kipper that – 'It's a Crippen, 'is mous*tache*!'
    But I'll 'ave do*mini*on – palm an' pine, an' meadowland an' marsh –
    In Tory Eras I shall rule, both meadowland an' marsh,
    Yes, the Lesser Breeds shall suffer, in town, meadowland an' marsh!

As critics wilt an' fide away, wi' their jargon an' their sneers,
I shall stand them Young Conservatives a multitude o' beers!
Blind obedience is me rule, *ideas* are wot I 'ates,
It's suff'rin' soldiers wot I loves, me rough tough *workin'* mates!
   Ow! It's Kipper this, an' Kipper that, an' ''E was keen on Him!'
   A *de*tergent omo-sex-u-al! But I'll mike their eyes go dim,
   The ones as thinks unclean o' me, I'll mike their eyes go dim!
   'Ighbrows, fairies, socialists – I'll mike their eyes go dim!

Home, Sweet Home!

'The cyanide – it was put in her tea – didn't reach Mrs Shaw,
but killed a house-cat.'

Ellery Queen, *The Adventure Of The Bearded Lady*

The American Language explicates everything –
a guest is a house-guest, a cat is a house-cat;
but every coat isn't a house-coat
nor every boat a house-boat.
You *could* have a house-mouse or a house-rat
but not a house-condor or a house-shark.
However much wildness and inexactitude are hated
not *everything* can be domesticated.

Sado-Masochism

(A Black Ballad)

'He lived with a prostitute of twice his age who enjoyed being
maltreated'
Colin Wilson and Patricia Pitman, *Encyclopaedia of Murder*, on Peter
Kürten, the mass-murderer of Düsseldorf.

There's something funny about the wimmin,
they seem to like violence of sorts
(though they don't really want to end up in the morgue
with all the other *mortes*).

Kürten would go out into the woods with
a simple servant girl –
he'd put his hands round her throat and say
'Why not? Let's give it a whirl!'

They didn't object, it seems, and what they
would give was a sexy giggle.
Sometimes he hit them with hammers or stabbed them –
no struggles. At most, a wriggle.

Heath was a drinker, and one of the boys,
the girls didn't think *him* bad.
He carved Margery Gardner, known in the underworld
as a notorious slapperad

and into bondage. And Doreen Marshall
was chased through the trees and slit –
she didn't want it, she was unlucky,
the female masochist bit.

But certainly German girls seemed to expect it
in the old pre-Hitler Twenties,
they thought it was normal, in no way kinky,
and they were quite compos mentis.

No one excuses these really horrible
male sadistic pigs –
but should the girls have met them half-way?
To pass them by like prigs

would have been safer, to say (like Puritans)
'Stuff your hammers and knives,
strangle *yourselves* if you must strangle somebody
and leave us alone, with our lives!'

NOTES   'Slapperad' is, or was, underworld slang for a
female masochist. Neville Heath was a big, strong handsome
man. He had fantastic success with women. Indeed it has been
suggested that he turned to sadism (late in his sexual career)
because he was bored with everything else. He was also a
confidence trickster and used to wear uniforms and medals to
which he was not entitled. He was executed in 1946 for the two
murders mentioned. Kürten, for murdering (at least) eight
women, was guillotined in 1931.

The Saints of the Suburbs

We are prized, we husbands – yes, we are prized.
Sometimes, when our coats are smooth and brushed,
we are allowed out.

Our arms are taken in the street, yes, we are prized.
We clean the car, we dig in the daffodils,
we photograph kids.

We are shown off in public – *Look what I got!*
And he's mine, all mine, like a mortgage!
A property, an investment.

We are boasted of, for other wives to wonder at.
Digby made the rabbit hutch and all the bookshelves!
A handyman, each of us!

We never drink too much or look at a secretary,
we are chauffeurs with sensory deprivation,
such saints of the suburbs!

Doctor Kildare

If Doctor Kildare
suddenly turned into
Doctor Darekill –
with his deadly hypodermic
and his lethal pill –
none of us would ever
dare to be ill!

Mrs Rat's Tea-Parties

(All honour to Ronald Firbank, born 17 January 1886,
died 21 May 1926)

At Mrs Rat's Tea-Parties
there are (velleities)
and diplomatic ladies in delicious gowns
widening their eyes at a stone-god's big-big . . . ???!!!
There is only a smattering of Hearties
(unless they have hyacinthine hair
like the more attractive Deities

or in other ways resemble a Donatello).
The 'prose' is out of Pater,
assez amusante! One might note a page or a faun
slyly 'at' the Heir Apparent's cool champagne . . .
while a vapid valse distracts a 'cello –
a weary music with a dying fall
and a 'Lost Boy' longing for Mater . . .

There *is* the sadness of the Peacocks' crying,
the last crow's-foot resting
beneath those eyes that are always-always tired.
My dear! The 'dialogue'! You can just see Evelyn,
imitative and more than a little trying,
'trying it on'! It's a (camp) comedy
no one's succeeded in besting . . .

and the mood music *can* be terrific
(about night, twilight, flowers),
it's all fabulous without a fable, mistily 'staged',
but even (Oh, the Sitwells!) on the edge of farce.
In his life, to be more specific,
he worked hard and certainly suffered
and all the pleasure is ours . . .

21 May 1986

Song: What We Are/Were Sentimental About

The Ancient World had seascapes
and very wonderful weather,
columns and architraves
and crucified slaves
and whips made of beautiful leather –
but no whisky or heather.

The Ancient World had flautists
whose music was so appealing,
dolphins and boys with curls
and qualified girls
who gave you a beautiful feeling –
but no cabers or reeling.

The Ancient World had dramas
to throw you right off your balance,
poets in togas who
until all was blue
read epics, with wine drunk in gallons –
but no ceilidhs or Lallans.

How to Write a Poem
in the American Style

Use the
two-word
line, en-
jambement,
etc.
where poss-
ible &
don't forget
the ampersand!

No need
for rhyme,
not much need
for rhythm –
it's all
like trying
to touch
your toes.
Anyone
can try it.

Campoets All!

Down the lanes of Literature, leafy Spring and Fall,
Come with me and sample the blossoms on the bough!
Nowhere is a leafier lane (where poets have a ball)
Than where those flowers of Cambridge show so fairly now –
Milton/Byron*/Tennyson/Empson!
Lamb poets, WHAM poets! Campoets all!

Ham poets, spam poets? Never, not at all!
Gray is there and, near him, his ploughman with his plough! –
Nashe and Marlowe flourishing – the flowers that never fall
Are Cambridge flowers simply, standing straight and tall –
Milton, Byron*/Tennyson/Empson!
Ram poets, BAM poets! Campoets all!

* Or substitute Wordsworth – according to taste. This poem
is dedicated, in a way, to all Professors of Poetry at Oxford.

A Scottish Psychiatrist Considers *La Bohème*

Of course, this opera is pre-Freud;
in 1896, when it was first produced
and Mimi first offered herself to be seduced,
Freud's main work was *Studies on Hysteria*
(1893). In collaboration with Breuer.
Would Giacosa and Illica have made Mimi coyer

if they'd ever read it? I think not.
Mimi, you remember, says she's lost *the key to her room.*
She looks for it *in the dark, with a man* – we assume
she deserves guid Scots words of trust and praise –
as one might say, a 'douce wee body'.
But she's not so douce – or as innocent as Noddy!

Later she tells Rodolfo the losing was sham.
She's a sly puss, a schemer, and that's
interesting; *Mimi* is what the French call pussycats.
(For us there's significance in a word like pussy.)
In those days Freud was only feeling his way –
but so was Mimi, we could, without contradiction, say.

Eddie Linden

(see 'Hohenlinden' by Thomas Campbell (1777–1844),
a poem once very popular in schools)

On Linden, when the sun was low,
The Polis* struck a bitter blow –
And from his lip the blood did flow,
    And from an eyebrow, rapidly!

Six stitches needed on the brow!
We cannot say exactly how
(The Force is quite a Sacred Cow
    And deals with suspects doughtily.)

We know they chucked him in a cell,
That he was drunk we know as well –
But why combine to give him Hell
    So bravely and with chivalry?

We've all been legless in our time,
Deep drunkenness is not a crime –
I'll bet a dollar to a dime
    That this was harmless revelry.

And if a man can hardly stand,
Why give him such a helping hand
To make him painfully to land
    In all the sleep of misery?

Of course we know the fighting drunk
Are more detested than a skunk,
But passing out, like doing a bunk,
    Is harmless stuff, like scenery.

* Scottish pronunciation, accent on first
syllable.

The combat deepens. On, ye Brave,
Who rush to glory, or the grave!
But *beating-up*, what fool or knave
    thinks that's the height of bravery?

Black eyes, romantic in old verse!
The guns, the fists, the looming hearse –
Though pigs feel better, we feel worse
    Beneath their shielding canopy!

Catflap Cats

Catflap cats are
latchkey children.
They're always
in or out –
rushing in for meals or
out to play in gardens.
That's what their life's
all about.

What Shall We Say of The British Council?

A Sea Shanty of 50 Years Ago
(Tune, roughly: *What Shall We Do With a Drunken Sailor?*)

What shall we say of the British Council,
what shall we say of the British Council,
what shall we say of the British Council
    early in the morning?

Tyrrell of Avon – then Lord Lloyd was Chairman,
he wasn't a soldier, sailor or airman –
but he really got in Lord Beaverbrook's hair, man,
    early in the morning!

That was the way with the British Council, etc.

He was as mischievous as St Trinian's
sent word to attack to his pulp dominions
(the papers that published his own opinions)
    early in the morning!

What did they say of the British Council, etc.

Remove coffee stains from harpsichords, boys,
how to – advice the Council affords, boys,
and that was *all*, said those primitive hordes, boys,
    early in the morning!

That's what they said of the British Council, etc.

Yes, Beaverbrook longed to run the Council,
as canaries long to munch up groundsel!
When you want a ton, a single ounce'll
    irk you in the morning!

So what can we say of the British Council, etc.

The Cou wants understanding, appreciation
of Britain abroad, through co-operation
(cult, ed., tech.) with every nation
    each and every morning!

That's what it wants, does the British Council, etc.

Spread the word, so that British Culture
shan't suffer premature sepulture,
the world be greedy as a vulture
    for British Life each morning!
Spread the word on the British Council, etc.

NOTE   When I worked for the British Council (1946–52) the folklore
was that when the Council was founded Lord Beaverbrook thought the
Chairmanship should have been his and, out of envy, gave orders that the
Daily Express should attack the Council every year when the Annual
Report was published. The 'story' that all the Council did was to tell
foreigners how to remove coffee stains from harpsichords actually
appeared in the *Express*.

Mr W.S.

You may have had syphilis
and your hair fallen out
or some of it (Verlaine
went in for such things),

did you have (Baudelaire)
a black woman for a mistress?
We guess you had a shrewlike
wife, big, a shouter,

older, a virago.

For these, your compensations:
Ben Jonson and the boys
thought you wrote the best
plays, as they were drinking,

in days when plays meant verse,
and the literary lordlings
admired your sugared
emblematic sonnets;

and of course, too,
you enjoyed the taverns,
a river not the Avon,
a large, important city

where you could be both
happy and unhappy,
be on your own,
and make by your scribbling

quite a bit of money.

The Victorian Singing

Yes, we had quite a large,
quite a large collation,
we discussed, yes, we discussed
several pork chops.
Some dozens of claret
were opened, were opened;
a pipe of port was in question,
in question.
Nobody was sober, was sober, was sober.
Lifted skirts, naked thighs, high boots.

All discussed, all discussed
in the lewdness of Latin!

But O for the oysters, oysters, oysters!

Chester

(Paean for a Perfect Idiot)

My favorite American cat is Chester –
and as a favorite he gets American spelling –
and it's in his praise that my organ is swelling!
But he's not the cat that would ever need belling* –
he's certainly not a criminal or a crumb
but he *is* a wee bit dumb!

He's genuine, not man-made or polyester
and he's mostly white, with very dark grey splotches –
if he were a fabric, you could match him, in swatches –
but he's far superior, by several notches;
raccoon-tailed, he's completely covered in *real fur*
and he sure knows how to purr!

He's never been a student – not even half a semester –
and his talent isn't for teaching or table-talking
but he's renowned everywhere for his way of walking;
with Tarquin's ravishing strides he goes by, stalking.
There's no need for brains in aristocrats –
Chester's a prize fool among cats!

New York, 16 April 1986

* 'Belling the Cat'. The old nursery story
describes how the mice try to put a bell on
the cat's neck, to warn of his approach.